PAMELA FREEMAN AND LIZ ANELLI
SEED to SKY
Life in the Daintree
AF604792
WALKER BOOKS
AND SUBSIDIARIES
LONDON • BOSTON • SYDNEY • AUCKLAND

Come to the **oldest forest** on Earth …
On the oldest continent …
Where the oldest trees reach
high into the sky …
We're going back into the past …

The Daintree Rainforest today covers more than 1200km² and is over 135 million years old – the oldest rainforest on Earth. The Daintree gets between 2000mm and 9000mm of rain each year, depending on where in the forest you measure. Before European settlement, the Daintree was much larger.

It's 200 years ago.

Watch out!

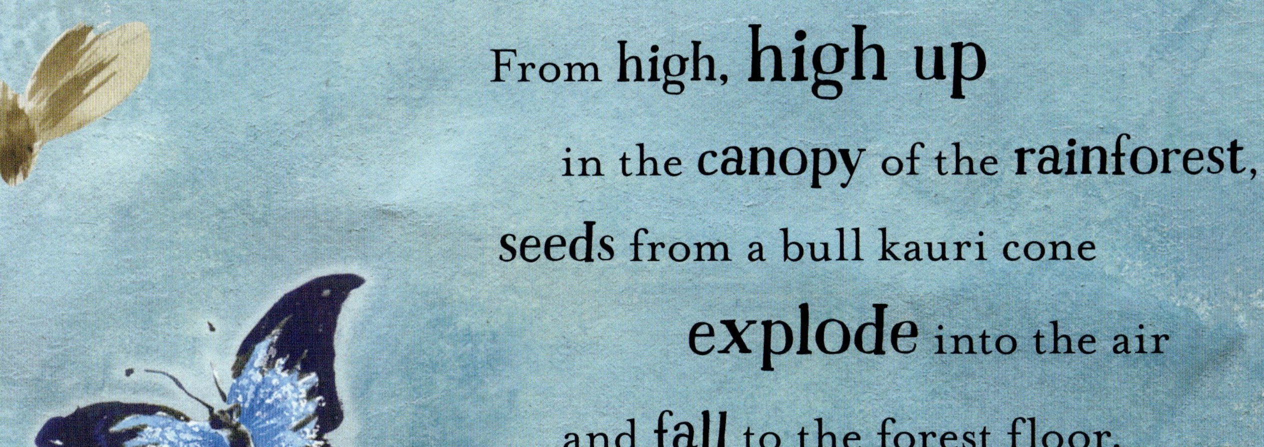

From high, **high up**

in the **canopy** of the **rainforest**,

seeds from a bull kauri cone

explode into the air

and **fall** to the forest floor.

Bull kauri conifers have been growing in Australia for more than 200 million years. They survived the extinction of the dinosaurs, and are one of the oldest tree species in the world. Full grown trees can be up to 600 years old.

Some of the delicious **seeds** are eaten.
One, by a Musky Rat-Kangaroo …

Others are pecked up by a bush turkey, which is frightened away by the 'whaap-whaap' of a Northern Barred Frog on the log nearby.

But one seed lies unnoticed ...

The kauri seed begins to **grow** ...

downwards.

Slowly, it forms **roots** underground, while platypuses play in the nearby creek, and the early-bird chowchillas whoop and whistle before scratching for worms under the **leaf litter.**

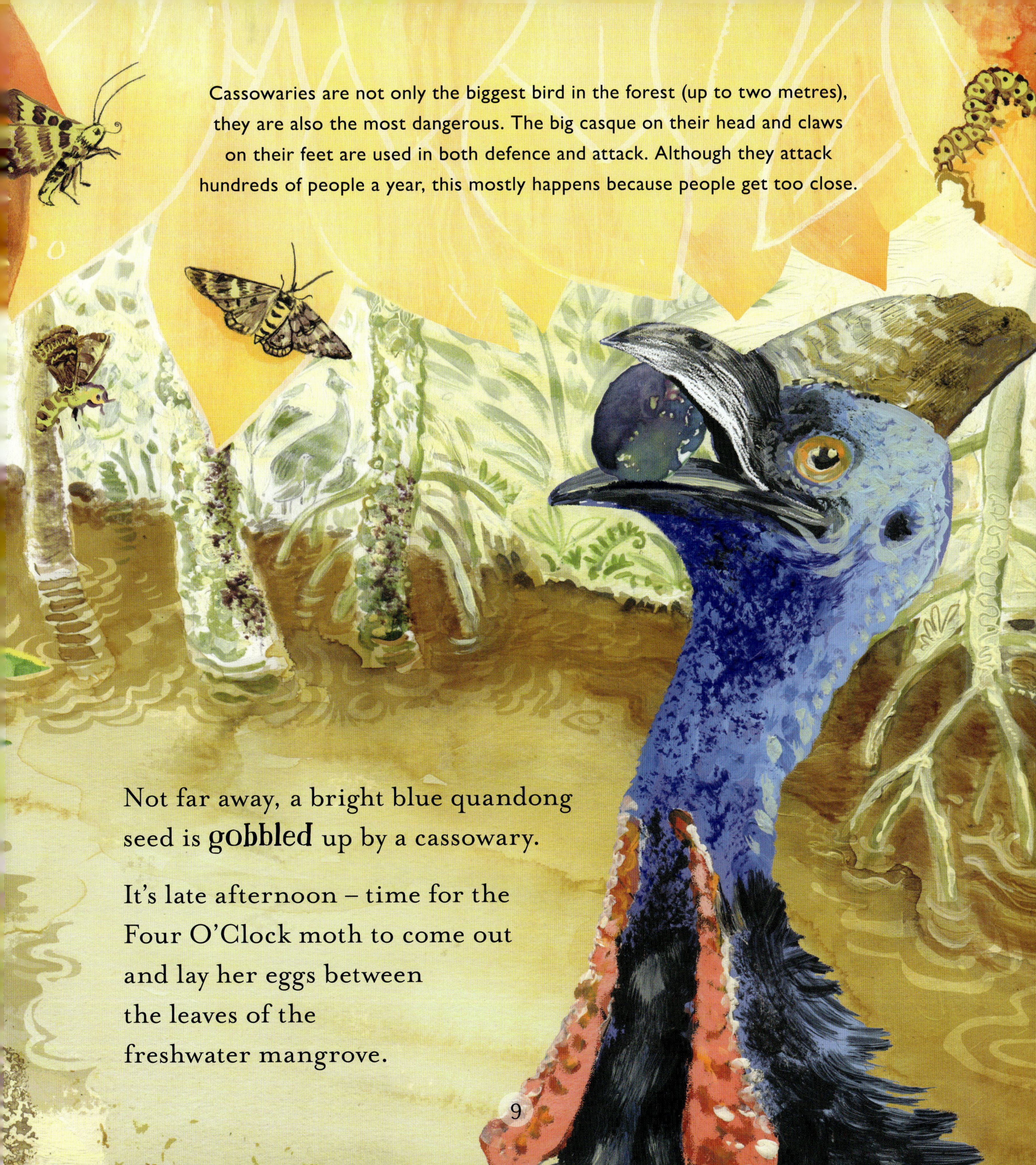

Cassowaries are not only the biggest bird in the forest (up to two metres), they are also the most dangerous. The big casque on their head and claws on their feet are used in both defence and attack. Although they attack hundreds of people a year, this mostly happens because people get too close.

Not far away, a bright blue quandong seed is **gobbled** up by a cassowary.

It's late afternoon – time for the Four O'Clock moth to come out and lay her eggs between the leaves of the freshwater mangrove.

The **Wet** has come, and **life-giving rain** seeps down to the bull kauri's roots. It begins to **shoot up**, until it pokes its tip out into the sweet air of the forest.

Look! Can you see?

The creek has **risen** and a Mouth Almighty swims past a school of rainbowfish and blue-eyes.

The Daintree Rainforest is a tropical forest, 16° south of the Equator. It has two main seasons, the Wet and the Dry. Cyclones are common during summer.

It's 190 years ago.

The bull kauri keeps **growing**,
struggling for light in the shade of the tall trees.

It's lunchtime! A dingo is on the scent of a bandicoot.
A Northern Water Dragon munches on a Rhinoceros beetle,
and a skink eats an Illawarra Plum.

Beetles are everywhere in the rainforest –
no one knows how many species there are.
New ones are frequently discovered.
Beetles make up around one-quarter
of all species on Earth!

The bull kauri is growing fast, becoming part of the **undergrowth.**

It puts out **cones**, as it will each year, ready to form seeds.

Noisy Pittas snap up snails near the creek, while the Red-Necked Crake wades in the shallows.

Butterflies are **everywhere!**

Blue Triangles,
swallowtails,
swordtails,
jezabels!

The Daintree has 230 species of butterflies, more than half the species found in Australia. Species from each of the five butterfly families can be found here.

It's 180 years ago.

The bull kauri is a **sapling** now, shooting up through the **understory** of the forest.

Look out! A lace monitor clambers over the Strangler Fig on a Bumpy Satinash, searching for birds' eggs, but the Wompoo pigeon parents protect their nest.

There are lizards all over the Daintree – from tiny skinks on the forest floor, to the huge lace monitors. Frill-necks, Boyd's Forest Dragons, and Northern Leaf-tailed Geckos … 22 species of skinks alone!

Seasons come and go …

Years pass …

It's 100 years ago.
The bull kauri keeps **growing.**
Kauri gum oozes from
slits in the trunk.

In the understory, beneath the **canopy** where the **rainforest** trees join their leaves in an unbroken cloud, a boobook owl hunts a Joseph's Coat moth.

Green fig parrots settle to sleep, and so do the fig wasps from their particular tree.

There are many kinds of fig trees in the Daintree, and each type of tree has its own species of wasp, which has evolved with the tree over millenia.

Several species of bats inhabit the canopy. They eat fruit, insects, or sometimes only nectar and pollen.

It's 50 years ago.

The bull kauri is 30 metres tall. Its next **challenge:** to fight its way through the thick canopy of trees **towards the sun.**

On the Bumpy Satinash next to it, baby Longicorn Beetles crawl out of the nest where they changed from larvae to beetles.

The Longicorn Beetle lays its eggs beneath the bark of the Satinash. The larvae feed on the tree, forming a hole. Once they change to beetles and leave the nest, black ants will move in. The ants protect the tree by eating the shoots of the vines which might otherwise strangle it. A good deal for the tree!

Far above the ground, the canopy

abounds with life.

Butterflies everywhere!

Can you see them sipping on the **nectar** of the Topaz Tamarind flowers? And birds: **thrushes** and **cuckoos**, **monarchs** and **whistlers**, **flycatchers** and **fantails**.

The Daintree area (including the coast) has more than 430 species of birds (Australia has around 830 species in total). Some of these live there all year round; others migrate from cooler areas for the summer.

As night falls on the **canopy**,
the **nocturnal** moths come out:
the Hercules moth, the Giant Wood moth,
the Night Citrus Swallowtail, and more.

Pythons sleep in the branches;
the white-lipped tree frog calls;
and the Eastern Tube-Nosed bat takes flight.

There are more moth species than butterflies in the Daintree, and they live at all levels of the rainforest.

Of the 10,000+ species of moths in Australia, most live in tropical rainforests.

It's ten years ago.

The bull kauri is 40 metres tall and 190 years old by the time its **crown** breaks through the canopy. Now it can drink in the sun and grow still taller.

A Ulysses butterfly perches on the very tip.

At the canopy level, the foliage of the mature trees interleaves to form a dense umbrella over the forest floor. There are birds, animals and insects which live their entire lives far, far above ground.

It's today!

The bull kauri is fully grown, almost 50 metres tall. Its dark green leaves reach out for the Spring sun. It flowers, and begins forming its **cones**.

Below, in the **Daintree** Rainforest,
animals, insects, reptiles and birds will thrive …
for as long as we **protect the forest.**

The Daintree is one of the great biodiversity sites of the world. The rainforest is much smaller than it used to be. Although it is now partially protected as a national park and World Heritage Site, some parts of it are privately owned, and vulnerable to exploitation.

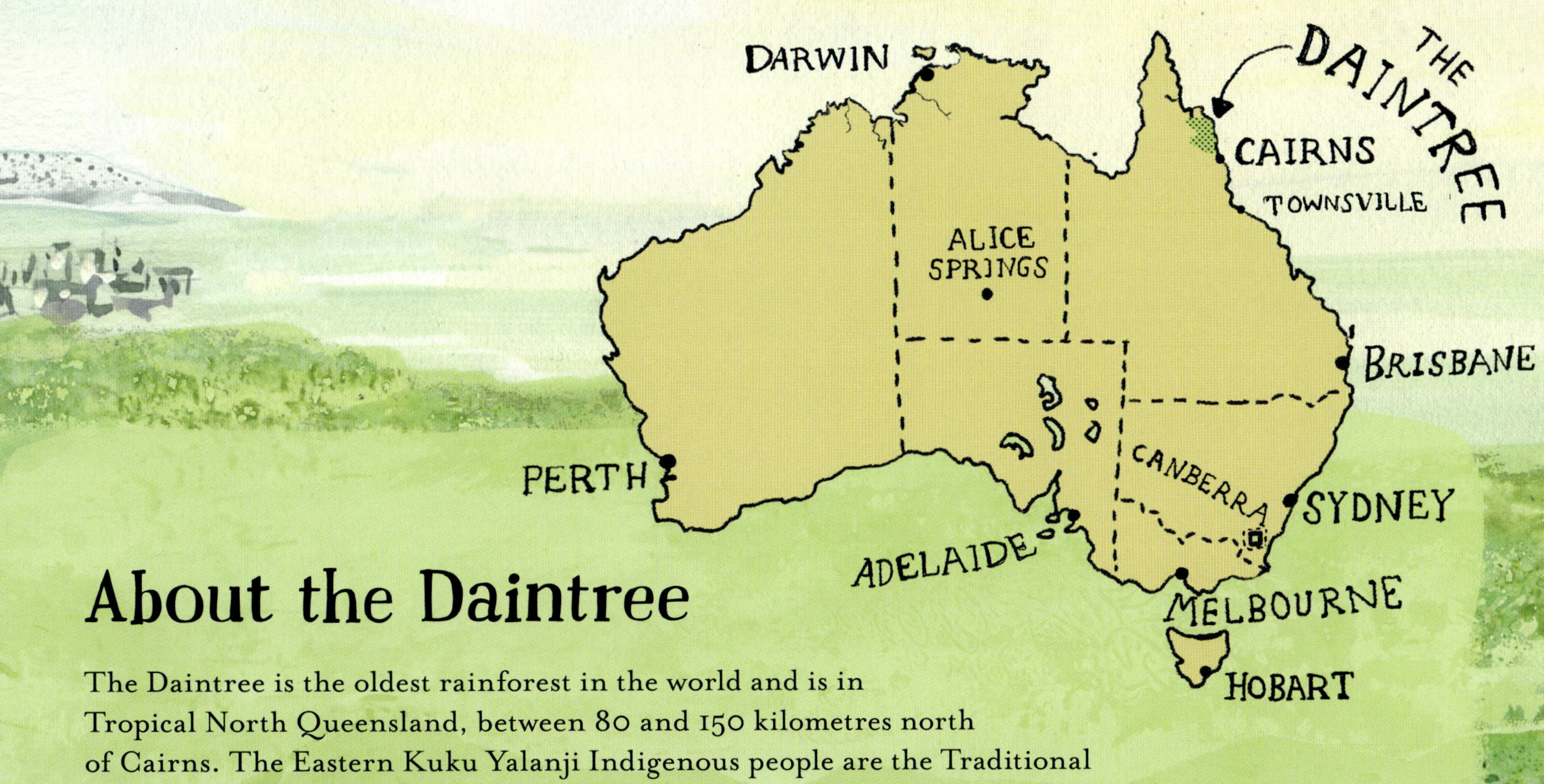

About the Daintree

The Daintree is the oldest rainforest in the world and is in Tropical North Queensland, between 80 and 150 kilometres north of Cairns. The Eastern Kuku Yalanji Indigenous people are the Traditional Owners of this area and have lived in this region for at least 50,000 years.

The Daintree is part of a much larger ecosystem: the Wet Tropics World Heritage Area, which spreads over 450 kilometres of the Queensland coastline. No one knows how the Daintree will respond to climate change, however, over the (at least) 130 million years of its life, there have been many periods where temperatures and conditions have changed. In those periods, animals and plants adapted and evolved to deal with the new conditions. Some went extinct; others thrived. We can expect the same thing to happen with the current changes in our climate.

Index

For Billy, Rory, and Harry – PF
To William T Cooper – LA

First published in 2024
by Walker Books Australia Pty Ltd
Gadigal and Wangal Country
Locked Bag 22, Newtown
NSW 2042 Australia
www.walkerbooks.com.au

This edition published in 2026

Walker Books Australia acknowledges the Traditional Owners of the country on which we work, the Gadigal and Wangal peoples of the Eora Nation, and recognises their continuing connection to the land, waters and culture. We pay our respect to their Elders past and present.

A catalogue record for this book is available from the National Library of Australia

ISBN: 978 1 761601 73 6

The illustrations for this book were created with mixed media
Typeset in Mrs Eaves and Mrs Ant
Printed and bound in China

EU Authorized Representative:
HackettFlynn Ltd., 36 Cloch Choirneal,
Balrothery, Co. Dublin, K32 C942, Ireland.
EU@walkerpublishinggroup.com

10 9 8 7 6 5 4 3 2 1